DEMONS

ANDREW CODDINGTON

Cavendish Square

New York

CREATURES OF FANTASY
Demons

BY

ANDREW CODDINGTON

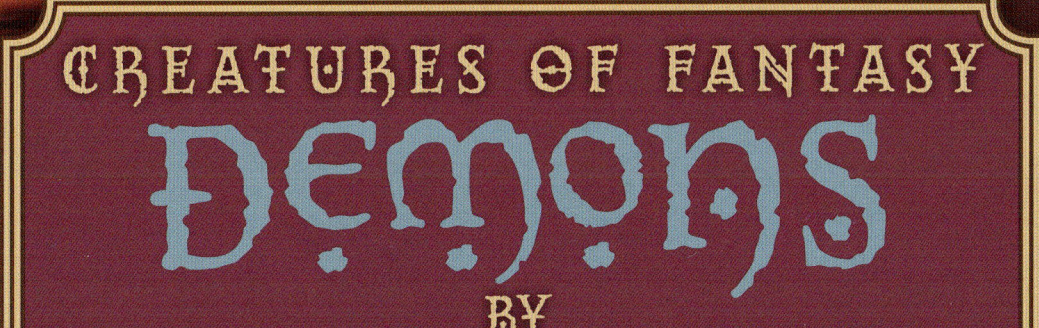

CAVENDISH SQUARE PUBLISHING · NEW YORK

Published in 2017 by Cavendish Square Publishing, LLC
243 5th Avenue, Suite 136, New York, NY 10016

Copyright © 2017 by Cavendish Square Publishing, LLC

First Edition

No part of this publication may be reproduced, stored in a retrieval system, or transmitted in any form or by any means—electronic, mechanical, photocopying, recording, or otherwise—without the prior permission of the copyright owner. Request for permission should be addressed to Permissions, Cavendish Square Publishing, 243 5th Avenue, Suite 136, New York, NY 10016. Tel (877) 980-4450; fax (877) 980-4454.

Website: cavendishsq.com

This publication represents the opinions and views of the author based on his or her personal experience, knowledge, and research. The information in this book serves as a general guide only. The author and publisher have used their best efforts in preparing this book and disclaim liability rising directly or indirectly from the use and application of this book.

CPSIA Compliance Information: Batch #CS16CSQ

All websites were available and accurate when this book was sent to press.

Cataloging-in-Publication Data

Names: Coddington, Andrew.
Title: Demons / Andrew Coddington.
Description: New York : Cavendish Square, 2017. | Series: Creatures of fantasy | Includes index.
Identifiers: ISBN 9781502618603 (library bound) | ISBN 9781502618610 (ebook)
Subjects: LCSH: Demonology--Juvenile literature.
Classification: LCC BF1531.C63 2017 | DDC 133.4'2--dc23

Editorial Director: David McNamara
Editor: Kristen Susienka
Copy Editor: Rebecca Rohan
Art Director: Jeffrey Talbot
Designer: Joseph Macri
Senior Production Manager: Jennifer Ryder-Talbot
Photo Research: J8 Media

The photographs in this book are used by permission and through the courtesy of: breakermaximus/Shutterstock.com, cover; Mary Evans Picture Library, 6, 14; Private Collection/Archives Charmet/Bridgeman Images, 8; Martin, John (1789-1854)/Louvre, Paris, France/Bridgeman Images 12; © Courtesy of the Warden and Scholars of New College, Oxford/Bridgeman Images, 13; Multiple/Unknown/Bodleian Libraries Shelfmark/Oxford (Public Domain) Digital Library/File: Kitab al-Bulhan --- devils talking.jpg - Wikimedia Commons, 16; Ayan82/Photolibrary/Getty Images, 19; DeAgostini/Getty Images, 20; De Agostini /Archivio J. Lange/Getty Images, 22; Orsel, Andre Jacques Victor (1795-1850)/Musee des Beaux-Arts, Lyon, France/Peter Willi/Bridgeman Images, 24; L' exorciste The exorcist de William Friedkin avec Linda Blair, Max Von Sydow, 1973/Bridgeman Images, 26; andreiuc88/Shutterstock.com, 28; Ravilious, Eric (1903-42)/© Fry Art Gallery, Saffron Walden, Essex, UK/Bridgeman Images, 30; REX/Newscom, 34; Teniers, David the Younger (1610-90)/Musee de la Chartreuse, Douai, France/Bridgeman Images, 35; Raphael (Raffaello Sanzio of Urbino) (1483-1520)/Louvre, Paris, France/Bridgeman Images, 36; High resolution scan by http://www.haltadefinizione.com/in collaboration with the Italian ministry of culture. Leonardo da Vinci (1452-1519) /File: Última CenaII.jpg - Wikimedia Commons, 39; Web Gallery of Art: Image (http://www.wga.hu/art/g/giotto/assisi/upper/legend/scenes_2/franc10.jpg) Info about artwork (http://www.wga.hu/html/g/giotto/assisi/upper/legend/scenes_2/franc10.html) File: Giotto (1266-1337) Arezzo.jpg - Wikimedia Commons, 40; Discovery via Getty Images, 41; Milwaukee Journal Sentinel/PSG/Newscom, 44; Fuseli, Henry (Fussli, Johann Heinrich) (1741-1825)/Detroit Institute of Arts, USA/Founders Society purchase with Mr and Mrs Bert L. Smokler/and Mr and Mrs Lawrence A. Fleischman funds/Bridgeman Images, 49; Dawn J Benko/Shutterstock.com, 50; World History Archive/Newscom, 52; Franco Origlia/Getty Images, 55; Darrell Wong/Fresno Bee/MCT via Getty Images, 57; Adam Berry/Redferns via Getty Images, 59.

Printed in the United States of America

CONTENTS

INTRODUCTION 6

ONE
AGENTS OF EVIL 9

TWO
DEMONS AROUND THE WORLD 15

THREE
DEMONIC POWERS 23

FOUR
THE DEMONS OF *DOCTOR FAUSTUS* 31

FIVE
BATTLING THE FORCES OF EVIL 37

SIX
DEMONS IN POPULAR IMAGINATION 45

SEVEN
DEMONS IN THE MODERN WORLD 53

Glossary 60
To Learn More about Demons 61
Bibliography 62
Index 63
About the Author 64

INTRODUCTION

Evil spirits known as demons have been blamed for people's torments and tragedies for centuries.

Since the first humans walked Earth, myths and legends have engaged minds and inspired imaginations. Ancient civilizations used stories to explain phenomena in the world around them, such as the weather, the tides, and natural disasters. As different cultures evolved, so too did their stories. From their traditions and observations emerged creatures with powerful abilities, mythical intrigue, and their own origins. Sometimes, different cultures encouraged various manifestations of the same creature. At other times, these creatures morphed into entirely new beings with greater powers than their predecessors.

Today, societies still celebrate the folklore of their ancestors—on-screen in TV shows and movies such as *Doctor Who*, *Once Upon a Time*, and *Star Wars*, and in books such as the *Harry Potter* and *Twilight* series. Some of these creatures existed, while others are merely myth.

In the Creatures of Fantasy series, we celebrate captivating stories of the past from all around the world. Each book focuses on creatures both familiar and unknown: the elusive alien, the grumpy troll, the devious demon, the graceful elf, the spellbinding wizard, and the harrowing mummy. Their various incarnations throughout history are brought to life. All have their own origins, their own legends, and their own influences on the imagination today. Each story adds a new perspective to the human experience and encourages people to revisit tales of the past in order to understand their presence in the modern age.

1

AGENTS OF EVIL

"Hell is empty, and all the devils are here."
WILLIAM SHAKESPEARE, *THE TEMPEST*

H UMANS HAVE ALWAYS HAD TO STRUGGLE with tragedy. From mass destruction as a result of natural disasters to the deaths of innocent people as a result of war, famine, and plague, tragedy is a part of the human experience. When faced with the reality of evil, we often wonder: where does it come from? Are all of these catastrophes random events, or are they actively caused by someone—or something?

For many people throughout history, it was clear what the origins of evil were. To them, evil was the result of conscious actions at the hands of supernatural beings whose goal was to torture and torment humans out of spite. These creatures have gone by many names, but they are most often called **demons**.

Opposite: In Christianity, demons are intent on corrupting human souls so that they may torture them for eternity in Hell.

Understanding Demons

The word "demon" comes from the Greek word *daemonium*, or "fiend." Daemonium shares the same root as the word for "divine power," which for the ancient Greeks was used to refer to most types of spirits and gods. The spirit of a deceased person, for example, would be considered a "demon" regardless of whether they were on Earth to do good or bad. Over time, the word "demon" came to refer only to spiteful supernatural entities. This caused some confusion among later scholars, who read ancient Greek works by writers such as Socrates and found them celebrating the *daemonia*, or demons. It seemed as if the pagan Greeks were worshipping demons. What they failed to understand was that the idea of demons as only **malevolent**, or evil, was a much later development.

Christianity has been the dominant religion in North America and Europe for centuries, so the notion of demons in those areas is largely based on Christian beliefs. Of the many divisions of Christianity that accept the existence of demons and sometimes even discuss the nature of them, the Roman Catholic religious tradition has an especially well-developed practice of **demonology**.

According to the Catholic Church, all demons were once angels made by God during the creation of the world. However, one of these angels, named Lucifer, grew jealous of humanity, whom God loved more than the angels. Lucifer was the first angel to disobey God's commandment to love humanity as He did. Today, Lucifer is sometimes called a "fallen angel" because he "fell" from God's favor. Along the way, he convinced one-third of God's angels to join him. As these angels rebelled against God, they became ugly-looking creatures. Their eagles' wings became the naked, bony wings of bats, and mottled, black flesh replaced their beautiful skin.

They transformed into demons. The demons followed Lucifer and waged a war against God. However, they lost and were banished to live in a place called **Hell**.

The Dark Lord of the Demons

In Catholicism, as in many religions, there are stories of demons at work in the world. However, all of these creatures take their orders from one supremely evil being: the **Devil**, also called Satan. The idea of a hierarchy, or ordering, of the demonic is an important belief in Roman Catholicism. The ranks of demons mirror the hierarchy, or order, of God and the angels. Satan can command the demons of Hell the same way God can command the angels of Heaven. On the one side is the goodness of God, on the other is the evil of the Devil, and in between is humanity, which is capable of doing both good and evil and is therefore a sort of battleground for the war for the human soul.

Hell: Homeland of the Demonic

The only place in God's creation that the defeated demons could go was Hell. Over the millennia, people had different ideas of what Hell actually was like, but most everyone who believes in it agrees that Hell is an unpleasant place to spend the afterlife. Many Catholic theologians envision Hell not as an actual place but as a state of spiritual being. Saint Thomas Aquinas, greatly respected in the Catholic faith, said that the human soul does not physically reside in a place after death but is in one of several states of spiritual being. The former leader of the Catholic Church, Pope John Paul II, wrote that one of those states is the complete absence of God, what the Catholic Church considers to be Hell.

Hell is often shown as a dark, terrifying place full of fire and despair.

However, the most popular definition of Hell has its roots in both the Bible and in pop culture. Many early Christians imagined Hell as an actual place, occupying the core of the Earth. This reflected the classical idea of a hierarchy of good and evil, with evil being low in the ground, goodness being high in the heavens, and humanity situated in between. The Book of Psalms, one of the books of the Bible, says that there was nothing but fire and brimstone—also known as sulfur, a product of volcanic eruptions—in Hell. Elsewhere in the Bible, in the Book of Revelation, Hell is imagined to be a lake of fire into which the souls of bad humans are thrown. Medieval writers added to this perception, depicting Hell as being full of horrifying torture devices controlled by demons. Today, movies such as Disney's *Hercules* envision Hell as a dark place below ground, full of fire, pain, and sadness. These thoughts perpetuate the notion that Hell is a place no one wants to spend much time in.

The Origin of Demons

Throughout history, there have been many instances where one religion is replaced by another, either because the believers of the old religion were converted—willingly or by force—or they were removed completely from the area where they lived. During this process, religions change. Sometimes, new believers adjust existing belief structures to fall more in line with their previous beliefs. Other times, the new religion must explain why it has replaced the old one.

This pattern of replacing old religions with new ones often leads to the creation of new demons. As the new religion moves in, worshippers see the beliefs of the old religion and, in order to explain why the old religion is wrong, they make demons out of the old religion's gods. An example of this is the Christian demon Beelzebub, a mutation of the Canaanite god Ba'al. Whereas the ancient Canaanites worshipped Ba'al, Christian theologians turned Ba'al into a negative figure. To them, Ba'al, or Beelzebub, was one of Satan's commanders in Hell, and worshipping him meant one had fallen into a trap set by the demon.

Imagining Satan

There are many different popular representations of the Devil. Perhaps the most identifiable of these is the red, horned man carrying a **pitchfork**. One of the first representations of the Devil carrying a pitchfork comes from a detail of Muiredach's High Cross, which is located in Monasterboice, County Louth, Ireland. Scholars speculate about the origin of the devil's pitchfork. Historian Jeffrey Burton Russell sees the similarity between the Devil's three-pronged pitchfork and the ancient Greek god Poseidon's trident. When Christianity replaced paganism as the dominant religion in Europe, the old gods of Greece and Rome were often considered demons, and thus the pitchfork came to be associated with the Devil.

Other scholars believe that the Devil's pitchfork may have a symbolic meaning. The pitchfork is a farming tool used during the harvest. In possessing a pitchfork, it seems that the Devil is here to harvest. However, instead of crops, the Devil's harvest takes the form of human souls.

Many representations of the Devil and demons feature pitchforks.

DEMONS AROUND THE WORLD

"The great dragon was hurled down—that ancient serpent called the devil, or Satan, who leads the whole world astray. He was hurled to the earth, and his angels with him."

Revelation 12:9

Demons are unique creatures because they are universal. There is a staggering variety of demons around the world. Nearly every culture—including all of the world's major religions—has some sort of concept of demons.

Demons of the Middle East

Few other parts of the world have had as big an impact on world history and culture as the Middle East. It is the birthplace of not only the world's first civilizations, but also of three of the world's major religions: Judaism, Christianity, and Islam. Given its

Opposite: Many cultures believe that demons reside in isolated places such as forests, where they may prey on unsuspecting travelers.

historical legacy, the cultures and religions of the Middle East have an incredibly rich and varied tradition concerning demons.

The earliest civilizations of the Middle East were situated in the area known as Mesopotamia, which includes the modern-day countries of Iraq, Kuwait, and Syria. The ancient Mesopotamians imagined that demons were forces of chaos that lurked on the outskirts of their new civilizations. In Mesopotamia, demons were responsible for natural disasters. Their favored haunts were in the wilderness. They were usually attached to certain places, such as desolate parts of the desert or in run-down, abandoned buildings. If a human wandered too far from the confines of civilization, the demons would descend on him or her, making the person sick or driving him or her insane.

This depiction of *djinn* dates back to the fourteenth century.

The Djinn: Demons of Islam

Islam's demons are known as ***djinn*** or *jinn*. Like humans, these beings were created by the god Allah with free will, but instead of being made of clay as humans were, the Qur'an (Islam's foundational text) says that djinn were made from fire without smoke.

One type of djinn is the genie, which appears in many legends, folktales, and even a Disney movie. The classic genie story is *Aladdin*, which tells the story of an orphaned boy who discovers a genie. According to the legend, Aladdin is recruited by a scheming sorcerer to retrieve a magical lamp from a cave, but the sorcerer traps him down there. When Aladdin finds the lamp, he tries to rub some dirt from its side when a genie appears. In rubbing the lamp, Aladdin frees the creature, who is bound to do Aladdin's bidding. In some genie stories, the genie grants the holder of the lamp three wishes. However, in many cases, these wishes turn out to have unintended consequences that do not work out well for the wisher.

Judaism

Demons have a complicated relationship in Judaism. To understand demons in Judaism, it is important to distinguish the different texts that serve as the foundation for the Jewish religion. The primary text in Judaism is the **Tanakh**, commonly considered the Bible of Judaism. In Exodus, one of the books in the Tanakh, it says, "You shall not tolerate a sorceress," including those who practice **witchcraft**. In the ancient Middle East, witches were thought to use demons to influence the world around them. Because demons were so closely associated with witchcraft, the prohibition of witchcraft of any kind, good or bad, meant that demons were irrelevant as far as the Tanakh was concerned.

In addition to the Tanakh, there are other related texts and movements in the Jewish religion. These texts are not necessarily canonical, meaning that they do not have authority over the religion's teachings. However, they do shed more light on other parts of the religion. The Talmud, which contains the collected works of Hebrew scholars through the centuries, as well as the mystical tradition known as Kabbalah, explore demonology in Judaism much more deeply. Jewish demonology, unlike Christian demonology, makes a distinction between good and evil demons. According to these traditions, demons are merely disembodied spirits looking for a host. Some of these spirits may be good, such as the spirit that animates a golem, a creature shaped from clay. Some Jews believe that Adam, the first man, was himself a golem. In the sixteenth century, a rabbi known as Maharal created a golem to defend the Jews living in a Prague ghetto from abuse at the hands of anti-Semites, or those who are prejudiced against Jews.

Other demons, known as *dybbuks*, were evil spirits. These spirits would wander the world looking for a human host to **possess**. After forcing their way into a host, they would torture the person, mentally and physically, and possibly murder him or her. In order to protect people, dybbuks had to be captured in specially blessed vessels, much like the magic lamps that held the genies of Arabia.

Demons of the East

While many civilizations may have had their roots in the Middle East, most people in the world now live in Asia. In fact, Asia has almost three times the population of Europe, North America, South America, and Australia combined. It also happens to be the world's largest continent. Asia is home to countless cultures, each living in unique environments, from the Tibetans in the heights of the Himalayas to the Japanese on their volcanic island in the Pacific Ocean. With such great diversity, it is no wonder that Asia is also home to a variety of unique perspectives on demons.

Hindu Demons

Hinduism is the world's third-largest religion after Christianity (first) and Islam (second). Despite its rank as third, Hinduism is nevertheless the world's oldest religion still being practiced today. The earliest recorded mention of Hinduism comes from 4,000 BCE. Over the millennia, Hinduism became one of the most complex religions, influenced by thousands of scriptures, and full of literally countless gods, demigods, spirits, and—of course—demons.

Demons in Hinduism are at times called *asura*, which can be both benevolent (good) and malevolent (evil), and **rakshasa**, who are all evil. Sometimes, asura and rakshasa are used interchangeably. Rakshasas have been brutal and fierce creatures since their creation. Traditional depictions of rakshasas show them as huge, ugly monsters. They have long fangs and claws for fingernails. Many stories about rakshasas describe how they hunt humans, sniffing out the scent of their flesh. When they come upon humans, rakshasas eat them, sometimes keeping their skulls as cups from which to drink blood.

Mara the Tempter

Similar to Christianity, Buddhism is a religion based on following the teaching and lifestyle of one uniquely holy man: Siddhartha Gautama, also known as the Buddha. Like Jesus Christ, the Buddha was tempted by an evil spirit trying to derail his journey to holiness. This evil spirit is known as Mara, which comes from the ancient Indo-European word for "to die." As the story goes, Mara appeared before the Buddha and tempted him with three beautiful women, saying that the Buddha could have them for brides if he wanted. In some accounts, the three women were Mara's daughters. Although the stories generally present them as being actual women, they happen to have names like "craving," "discontent," and "attachment," three feelings that Buddhists believe stand in the way of achieving holiness. Buddha could not be distracted by the women; however, practicing Buddhists are told to look out for the temptations of Mara and his daughters.

A typical Hindu *rakshasa*.

Japanese *oni* can be both tormenting as well as protective spirits.

The Oni: Demons of Japan

The Japanese have a rich tradition around demons, which they call *oni*. One reading of the Japanese character for oni suggests that the meaning of the word is derived from the word "hiding," or concealing. The first oni were invisible entities responsible for large-scale tragedies, such as tsunamis, earthquakes, and plagues. Eventually, people in Japan began to imagine oni as having physical form. To match their terrifying reputation as agents of evil, oni are often depicted as grotesque creatures. Like classical Western demons, oni usually have a red body and horns. Additionally, some oni are said to be taller than 50 feet (15.24 meters), have many eyes, and can sometimes change their shapes.

One such oni haunts Agi Bridge. There is a legend about a man who bragged that he was not afraid of the demon reportedly living there. When he started to cross it, he met a woman, but as soon as their eyes locked, she transformed into a huge, green ogre and chased after him. The man escaped, but the demon found where he lived. The demon again changed shape, appearing in the form of the man's brother. When the demon knocked on the man's door, the man unknowingly let it in. The demon attacked him and ultimately killed him, biting off his head and parading it before his family before vanishing into the night.

Oni are not simply all evil, however. Although capable of spreading evil and horror, oni are also protective spirits. Statues of grotesque oni, for example, are placed in front of buildings to keep out unwanted spirits, similar to Western gargoyles.

Lilith: Terror in the Night

Although there is little mention of demons in the Hebrew Tanakh, demons were a part of everyday life for the ancient Hebrews. One of the few demons that is mentioned in the Tanakh was known as Lilith. The Hebrew word *lilit*, which is the root for the name Lilith, has a variety of meanings, including "night creature" and "screech owl" (in many cultures, screech owls are associated with death and evil because of their high-pitched whine, their ability to fly silently, and their practice of hunting at night). Given her name, Lilith was imagined to be a demon that was active at night. Some legends say that she was a type of demon known as a **succubus**, who hurt men while they slept. Other stories say that Lilith often broke into houses late at night to steal children.

Lilith has been the object of imagination in not just Judaism but many other cultures for millennia. Much was made of Lilith in the nineteenth century, when Europeans chose her as the subject of paintings and writings. In these, Lilith is often depicted as being alluringly beautiful, representing the dangerously seductive power of women.

In modern times, Lilith has been taken up as a mascot for many feminist groups. These groups argue that Lilith is one of countless symbols that has been used to reinforce unfair and untrue gender stereotypes about women. In 1997, the female vocalist Sarah McLachlan instituted a touring music festival comprising women vocalists and women-led bands. This was called Lilith Fair. The point of the festival was to bring positive attention to women and their contributions to music and society.

3

DEMONIC POWERS

"I will come to you in the black of some terrible night, and I will bring a pointy reckoning that will shudder you. And you know I can do it ... I have seen some reddish work done at night, and I can make you wish had never seen the sun go down!"

ARTHUR MILLER, *THE CRUCIBLE*

As AGENTS OF EVIL, DEMONS ARE blamed for a number of tragedies. These range in scale from individual terrors to wide-scale destruction. Many cultures throughout history thought that demonic spirits were responsible for such things as plagues and natural disasters. Witches that had sold their souls to the Devil were also thought to be able to harness these powers.

Tormenting Humans

As destructive as demons can be, many demons seem intent on one thing: tormenting a single person. This desire may stem from the Christian perception of the creation of the Devil and demons.

Opposite: Grotesque demons delight in torturing human souls, as demonstrated in this eighth-century Christian relief.

Their jealousy of God's preference for humans was the source of their ultimate suffering in Hell, so demons want to get revenge on humans. One of the ways demons do this is by distorting reality. Many stories about demons mention that they have the ability to lie to a person or otherwise keep them from seeing the truth. William Shakespeare addresses the nature of lies and misdirection in his play *The Merchant of Venice:*

> The devil can cite Scripture for his purpose.
> An evil soul producing holy witness
> Is like a villain with a smiling cheek,
> A goodly apple rotten at the heart.
> O, what a goodly outside falsehood hath!

Demons might tempt humans toward evil with arguments that often seem to make sense.

Taken literally, this quote means that evil people and demonic spirits may use things that are good in order to further their diabolical ends. Using something people see as good, such as holy scripture, lends a demon credibility and makes people more likely to trust what it's saying. However, the demon is merely spreading a distortion of the truth.

Related to their desire to trick and deceive humans through lies, demons are also thought to be able to change form. Demons have been imagined in art, literature, and modern film in many different ways, from the ugly, bat-winged monsters that were common in the Middle

Ages to human forms popular in modern representations of the Devil and demons.

Demons also have the ability to grant wishes, as with the case of genies. In many stories, asking a demon to grant a wish turns out to be a cautionary story, in which the person wishes for one thing but receives something else or must suffer from unintended consequences. Demons in these stories seem to be content with spreading chaos or pulling tricks. In the West, where demons are generally ruthless and evil, demons bargain. A common form of bargaining in demon lore is trading a person's soul for something the person wants in the mortal world, such as power, wealth, love, or talent. During a short time, the person may enjoy the benefits of their bargain, but the demon always comes back to claim their end of the deal: an eternity of suffering for the bargainer.

Possession

Perhaps a demon's most terrifying ability is to possess, or take control of, a person. Demons are spiritual beings, which gives them the capability to enter someone's body and control their actions. When this happens, the person is at the mercy of the demon, and their own spirit becomes trapped within the body. There are many cases of demon possession recorded in the Bible. In the Gospel of Mark, there is a young boy who falls prey to a demon: "who, wheresoever he [the demon] takes him [the young man], dashes him, and foams, and gnashes with his teeth, and pines away … and oftentimes he cast him into fire and into waters to destroy him."

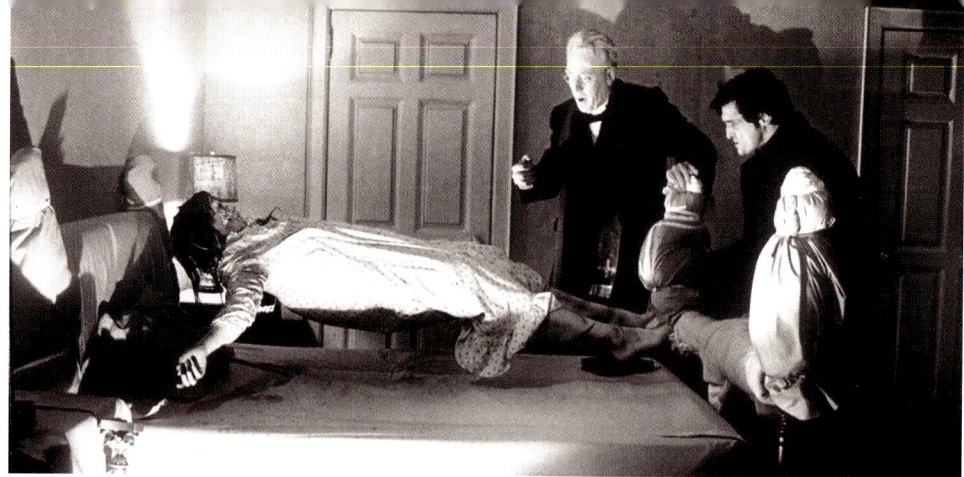

A scene from the movie *The Exorcist*.

Symptoms of Possession

Just as with someone suffering from a disease, someone who is possessed by a demon might show certain conditions that are shared across different cases. These are called symptoms. One common symptom of demonic possession is speaking in tongues. "Tongues" are foreign languages that may either be a real, actual language, or some unknown language commonly thought to be the language of Hell. Some alleged victims of possession are reported to have the ability to speak perfect Latin, for example, even though they have never before studied the language. Other symptoms might include strange, sudden, and unnatural body movements, such as eyes rolling in the back of the head, loss of control of limbs, erratic movement of the head, and so on.

A person under the effects of demonic possession may also be capable of superhuman abilities. In addition to the story of the young man, the Gospel of Mark includes another story of a man possessed by a demon who lived in a graveyard. While under the effects of the demon, the man experienced inhuman strength. Whenever his neighbors tried to tie him up, he burst through the chains, and they could not keep him down.

A case of demonic possession may not only manifest in strange behavior in the person but also unexplained occurrences on physical objects around him or her. This might mean the shaking and movement of furniture, sounds of scratching late at night, and—in extreme cases—appearances of strange fluids including blood on the walls and floors.

In some cases, however, the best way to confirm that someone has been possessed is to simply ask. The first-century CE Christian theologian Tertullian wrote that a spirit will confess to being demonic if it is asked directly by faithful Christians.

Doubts About Possession

Although many religions acknowledge the reality of demonic possession, skeptics that do not believe in spirits, good or evil, often deny the possibility. These people often turn to psychology to explain symptoms of demonic possession. It's important to note that demonic possession is not included in *Diagnostic and Statistical Manual of Mental Disorders*, the accepted authority on mental health issues provided by the American Psychiatric Association. To many, this would signify that demonic possession is not a true illness. Second, many well-documented mental disorders, such as **schizophrenia**, have symptoms that closely resemble those of alleged cases of demon possession. These include delusions, speaking in tongues, or reacting violently.

To further the skeptics' approach, there have been cases of so-called "possessions" that were successfully treated not through divine means but through medication and rehabilitation by trained mental health professionals. This suggests that demonic possession has a modern explanation and cure. Nevertheless, not every case of alleged demonic possession has been healed through medical means. There remain some cases where a more spiritual approach, such as through prayer, worked when medical treatment did not.

The wendigo is an evil spirit said to haunt lonely, wild places.

The Wendigo: Demon of the North East

Before European colonists arrived in North America, the lands around the Great Lakes were occupied by several Native tribes. Many of these cultures shared a legend about a demonic spirit that haunted the lonely woods in the north. This spirit was called the wendigo. The wendigo is a spirit capable of possessing humans. Some stories report that the wendigo can possess a person in their dreams, but most say that a person falls prey to the wendigo if they eat human flesh. To eat human flesh is a serious taboo in many Native tribes, even in cases where doing so is the only way to survive. These cultures thought it was better to starve to death than to eat a fellow human being, because to do so would turn a person into an even worse monster.

The Algonquin of the eastern parts of Canada and the United States called the wendigo the "spirit of lonely places." From wild forests to desolate mountains, these lonely places refer not only to the favored haunts of the creature but also to places where one might be tempted to resort to cannibalism and thereby fall prey to the spirit of the wendigo.

Once possessed by the wendigo, legend says, the person mutates into a horrifying creature. Accounts differ as to the wendigo's appearance. Some believe the wendigo looks like Bigfoot. Others say the wendigo resembles a werewolf. Still others imagine a completely different creature, one with glowing eyes, claws, and horns like a moose. Regardless of what it looks like, all stories agree that the wendigo has an insatiable hunger for human flesh. The wendigo has often been blamed for mysterious disappearances up through the twentieth century, and sightings stretch from eastern Canada all the way west to the Rocky Mountain range in the western United States. The wendigo's influence continues today: the creature makes an appearance in the horror game *Until Dawn* (2015).

THE DEMONS OF DOCTOR FAUSTUS

*"Why this is hell, nor am I out of it.
Think'st thou that I, who saw the face of God,
And tasted the eternal joys of heaven,
Am not tormented with ten thousand hells
In being deprived of everlasting bliss?"*

Christopher Marlowe, Doctor Faustus

Because demons are so universal and have such a long history dating back to the early millennia BCE, there are countless stories, myths, and legends about demons. One story that has had a huge influence on later conceptions of demons is the play *Doctor Faustus*. *Faustus* was written by an English playwright named Christopher Marlowe, who lived in the second half of the sixteenth century. As a contemporary of Shakespeare, Marlowe's acting company competed with the Bard himself. Marlowe was so talented, in fact, that many who argue that Shakespeare could not have been a real playwright believe that it was Marlowe who wrote many of the plays attributed to Shakespeare.

Opposite: An illustration from the play of *Doctor Faustus*.

The Tragical History

The Tragical History of the Life and Death of Doctor Faustus tells the story of Dr. Faustus, an incredibly talented and well-educated German scholar. When the play begins, Faustus expresses his frustration at exhausting every subject of scholarship known to man. He has mastered the logic of the ancient Greeks and the laws of the ancient Romans. He has studied medicine, astronomy, mathematics, and even theology. Despite this impressive accomplishment, Faustus wants even more, but he has nowhere left to go with conventional studies. He seeks, as he says, "a greater subject [to] fitteth Faustus' wit." However, he comes upon a book on the topic of **necromancy**, or black magic, which seems to hold the knowledge he desires.

Faustus is filled with delusions of even greater success, wealth, and power. He reads through the book and learns about its evil spells. By cursing God and revoking his Christian baptism, Faustus summons a demon by the name of Mephistopheles.

Through Mephistopheles, Faustus negotiates a bargain with Lucifer, the king of the demons. Lucifer agrees to give Faustus unlimited power for twenty-four years. During this time, Mephistopheles will serve as Faustus's personal servant. At the end of it, Lucifer is free to claim Faustus's soul. In order to seal the agreement, Faustus must sign with his blood. When he cuts his arm, however, it miraculously closes itself while a heavenly voice warns Faustus, *"Homo fuge!"* ("Man, flee!"). Faustus ignores the warning, cutting his arm again and binding his bargain.

For the next twenty-four years, Faustus spends his time on vain enjoyment. He first summons fresh fruits in the thick of winter. Later, he summons the spirit of Helen of Troy, the most beautiful woman who ever lived, according to Greek mythology. Helen becomes his wife. From there, Faustus lords his power over the German emperor and the pope. In one scene, he pranks the pope and the cardinals by becoming invisible and stealing their dinner plates while they eat.

At several points, Faustus grows tired of what are largely wasted talents—after all, conjuring spirits and pulling juvenile pranks were not what he imagined would be the benefits of selling his soul. At these moments, angels come to Faustus and implore him to revoke his agreement with the Devil. Each time Faustus comes close to doing so, Mephistopheles distracts Faustus with some new trick.

At the end of the play, Faustus's contract has run its course. On the eve of his final day, Faustus finally begins to grasp the seriousness of his deal. The clock in his chamber marks each hour as he comes closer and closer to his fate. Faustus looks around desperately for the salvation that had been offered to him by the angels for the entire play, but it is nowhere to be found:

> Yet for Christ's sake whose blood hath ransomed me,
> Impose some end to my incessant pain.
> Let Faustus live in hell a thousand years,
> A hundred thousand, and at last be saved.

As the clock strikes midnight, Mephistopheles and a horde of other demons appear to Faustus in a storm of thunder and lightning. They tear his body apart and drag his soul down with them.

Actor Jude Law plays the title role of *Doctor Faustus* in a 2002 London production.

Influence of *Faustus*

The story of Doctor Faustus has had an enormous impact on Western ideas about the Devil, demons, and **damnation**. Many of its symbols and themes have been carried over into other stories. For example, before Faustus makes his deal with the Devil, an angel and a demon appear on either side of him and make the case to either save his soul or to sell it. This scene has grown into the popular representation of an angel on one shoulder and a demon on the other. The idea that angels and demons appear on a person's shoulders to discuss his or her behavior has been copied countless times. It is particularly popular in cartoons, because it is widely recognized as a way to signify internal conflict. The shoulder angels have appeared in modern TV shows like *The Simpsons* and *Looney Toons*, and in movies, such as Disney's *The Emperor's New Groove*.

Additionally, *Doctor Faustus* has given rise to the idea that a person can sell his or her soul in exchange for certain earthly pleasures or successes. This theme, which has become very common in stories about demons, is so closely associated with *Doctor Faustus* that it is known as the "Faustian bargain."

A seventeenth-century painting showing witchcraft and sorcery.

Demons and Sorcery

The premise of *Doctor Faustus* is based on the longstanding idea that powers of sorcery and witchcraft come from the manipulation of spirits, including demons. Sorcerers and witches have been associated with spirits since the civilizations of Mesopotamia. It used to be that witches could be either good or bad depending on what sorts of spirits they relied on to carry out their wishes. When Judaism made a prohibition of all sorcery (witchcraft) in the Torah, and Christianity, which largely grew out of Judaism, adopted the same perspective, witches came to be seen as evil as the demons they called upon—and were feared just as much.

Fear over witches reached its peak in America between 1692 and 1693, when the town of Salem and surrounding areas of Massachusetts were rocked by accusations of witchcraft. Informed by their Puritan theology that Satan was active in daily life, people grew paranoid and suspicious about their neighbors' behavior. Many residents of Salem came forward with testimony that they had seen the accused witch talking to the Devil. Many claimed to have seen the accused sign the Devil's Book. By doing so, the witch pledged her soul in exchange for demonic powers to cause pain, sicken, and even kill.

The Salem witch trials, as they became known, were responsible for the execution of nineteen people, all but one of them women. It is remembered as one of the darkest moments in American history.

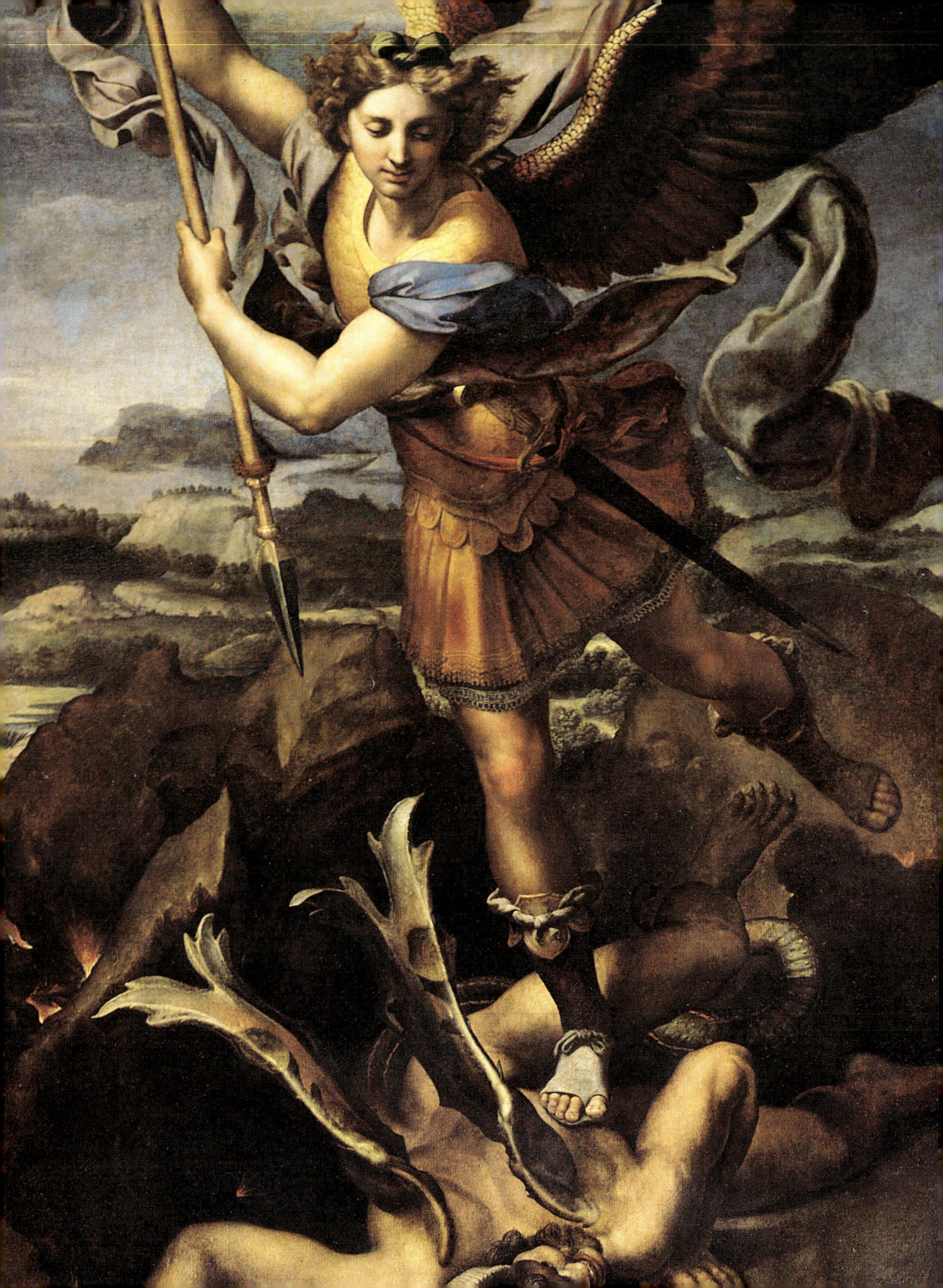

5

BATTLING THE FORCES OF EVIL

"I think the point is to make us despair.
To see ourselves as … animal and ugly.
To make us reject the possibility that God could love us."

FATHER MERRIN, *THE EXORCIST*

DEMONS ARE A REAL THREAT IN MANY cultures. Humanity's flawed nature makes humans susceptible to attack from evil forces on a daily basis. Even the holiest people may be targeted, so many people have come up with means to protect themselves and others from demonic spirits.

Purification Rituals

Different cultures have their own specialized means of protecting against demons. Demons are said to be repelled by certain objects, such as a crucifix or holy water in the Roman Catholic religion. Other Christian denominations will also bless individuals and homes to keep evil spirits out. Many Native American tribes

Opposite: Many Christians believe that God and the angels have been fighting demons since the beginning of time.

practice a ritual known as smudging, which involves the burning of dried white sage, a type of bushy plant. Practitioners set fire to the sage and sweep the smoke over their heads and around their bodies in a washing motion. This is thought to cleanse the person's body and home of any bad spirits.

There are also several folk remedies to keep demonic spirits at bay. Ancient people once thought that salt repelled demons. In order to protect a house, for example, a family might sprinkle a line of salt on thresholds and windowsills. This is thought to create a protective barrier that demons cannot cross. There is some debate as to why this is, but one of the most common explanations is religious. Jesus once told his disciples that they are the "salt of the earth," indicating that salt was sacred. Salt is also used to make holy water in the Roman Catholic religious tradition. Another more figurative reason has to do with the way salt was used in ancient times. Before refrigerators, early humans used salt to preserve meat. This quality of salt led people to use it as a symbol for things that last, such as friendship, love, and holiness.

The importance of salt also gave rise to the popular superstition around spilling this sacred condiment. Medieval Europeans believed that Judas Iscariot, who betrayed Jesus, spilled a shaker of salt at the Last Supper (this scene even made its way into Leonardo DaVinci's painting *The Last Supper*, where Judas is seated third from the left of Jesus and is shown knocking over a saltshaker with his arm). If a person tips over a saltshaker, it is thought to invite evil spirits to one's location. In order to repel these demons, one must pinch some of the spilled salt in their right hand and toss it over the left shoulder, where people commonly thought the Devil's face appeared.

Judas (*seated second from left*) spills a shaker of salt (*circled*) in Da Vinci's *The Last Supper*.

Combating Possession

Although there were many ways of proactively protecting against demons, sometimes it was not enough. What could be done when a demon had already invaded someone's body and was possessing them? Religions and cultures have come up with many unique forms of driving a demon out of a person's body. Because possession is thought to be a spiritual ailment, many of these means are spiritual in nature. These often include long hours reciting prayers, performing complex purification rituals, and demands made by priests and other spiritual representatives to the demon to vacate the person's body.

The Catholic Church has one of the most regimented rituals for removing a demonic spirit from a person's body. This ritual is known as the Rite of **Exorcism**, commonly known simply as an exorcism.

Before an exorcism can be performed, it must be approved by the Vatican, the governing body of the Catholic Church located in Rome. The Vatican must review the request for exorcism. The person who is alleged to be possessed must first go through physical and psychological evaluations. This is to prevent exorcisms from being performed for people who simply have a treatable medical problem and are not actually under the influence of demons. The

Here, St. Francis expels evil spirits from the city of Arezzo, Italy.

Catholic Church may also look for other unexplainable phenomena consistent with possession, such as speaking in tongues or mysterious movement of furniture. Other aspects the Catholic Church considers includes evidence related to religion. For example, if a person is unusually blasphemous (meaning they speak about God disrespectfully) or sacrilegious (meaning that they deliberately and offensively misuse sacred objects), the Catholic Church is more likely to believe that a demon is involved. Once the Vatican is satisfied that the case is one of an authentic demonic possession, it will authorize specially qualified priests to perform the ritual. The priests must also have the approval from the bishop of the diocese in which the exorcism will be performed.

Since demons naturally don't play by the same rules that humans have set for themselves, the demon may force the victim to violently lash out at those trying to drive out the demon. In this case, the exorcism may begin with restraining the victim. This is to keep the person from harming his- or herself or others around him or her. While restrained, though, the demon may verbally abuse the exorciser, thereby trying to get them to retaliate. From there, the priests lead a special course of prayer, which is outlined in a document called the *Rituale Romanum* (Roman Ritual). This process includes the saying of prayers, pleas to holy figures within the Catholic Church known as saints to intervene on behalf of the victim, and finally commandments to the evil spirit to leave the person's body. The Catholic Church believes it is essential that an exorcism must be completed once it has begun; otherwise, the demon may be released into the world to cause havoc.

The Exorcism of Roland Doe

The most famous case of an actual exorcism occurred in the 1940s and spanned the states of Maryland and Missouri. The target of the possession was a teenager called Roland Doe. "Roland Doe" is a pseudonym, or false name, which was created to protect the boy's identity. Other accounts list the boy's name as Robbie Mannheim. The event was so famous that it served as inspiration for one of the most famous and terrifying books (later made into a movie) about demonic possession: *The Exorcist.*

It is speculated that Doe fell under the influence of a demonic spirit after playing with a Ouija board. Also known as a "spirit board," a Ouija board is a device used to communicate with spirits. Ouija boards feature the letters of the alphabet; numbers; and

This house in St. Louis, Missouri, is the site of one of the most well-documented and frightening cases of demonic possession and exorcism.

simple phrases like "yes," "no," and "goodbye." They come with a pointer, which is held loosely by two or more people, the idea being that a spirit may use the energy of the participants to move the pointer. By asking simple questions, the participants can have a basic conversation with a spirit.

After playing with the Ouija board, Doe's family started to experience strange phenomena, including the sound of scratching on the walls and floors and the shaking of Doe's bed. Eventually, scratch marks started to appear on the boy's skin. The family took Doe to Georgetown University Hospital, but the doctors could not find anything medically wrong with him. Worried that something more sinister was at work, the family sought help from the Catholic Church. The **Jesuits**, a religious order within the Catholic Church, were called in to help.

Doe's exorcism began at his home in Maryland, but it could not be completed. During the ritual, Doe became extremely violent. He is said to have broken free from one of his restraints and broken off a bedspring, which he used to slash the priest's arm and interrupt the exorcism.

Doe's family moved him to a relative's home in St. Louis, Missouri. Over the course of several weeks, nine Jesuit priests attempted to exorcise Doe. The ordeal became more dangerous as time went on. Doe shook his bed violently while three men held him down. He grew verbally abusive, and one of the priests reported burns like cattle brands that appeared on the boy's body. These burns said things like "hello" and "evil." An image of the Devil even appeared on Doe's thigh at one point. Eventually, Doe fell into a convulsion when one of priests commanded the demon to leave Doe. When Doe came to, he said, "He is gone!"

Father Halloran, one of the priests who helped exorcise Doe, reported that he led "a rather ordinary life" after the event. When historian Thomas B. Allen wrote a book about Doe's encounter, he reached out to him twice, but Doe never responded. It seems he only wanted to put the ordeal behind him. To this day, Catholics in Prince George's County, Maryland, act out the Crucifixion of Christ in Doe's neighborhood in the hopes of keeping the evil spirit at bay.

Dangers of a Ouija Board

Ouija boards have a reputation for being extremely dangerous. Many people believe that Ouija boards open portals to "the other side"—the spirit world—but that human beings can never be sure of who exactly is coming through that portal. Someone using a Ouija board may think that they're communicating with a deceased loved one—or they may be welcoming a demon who is only pretending to be a friend.

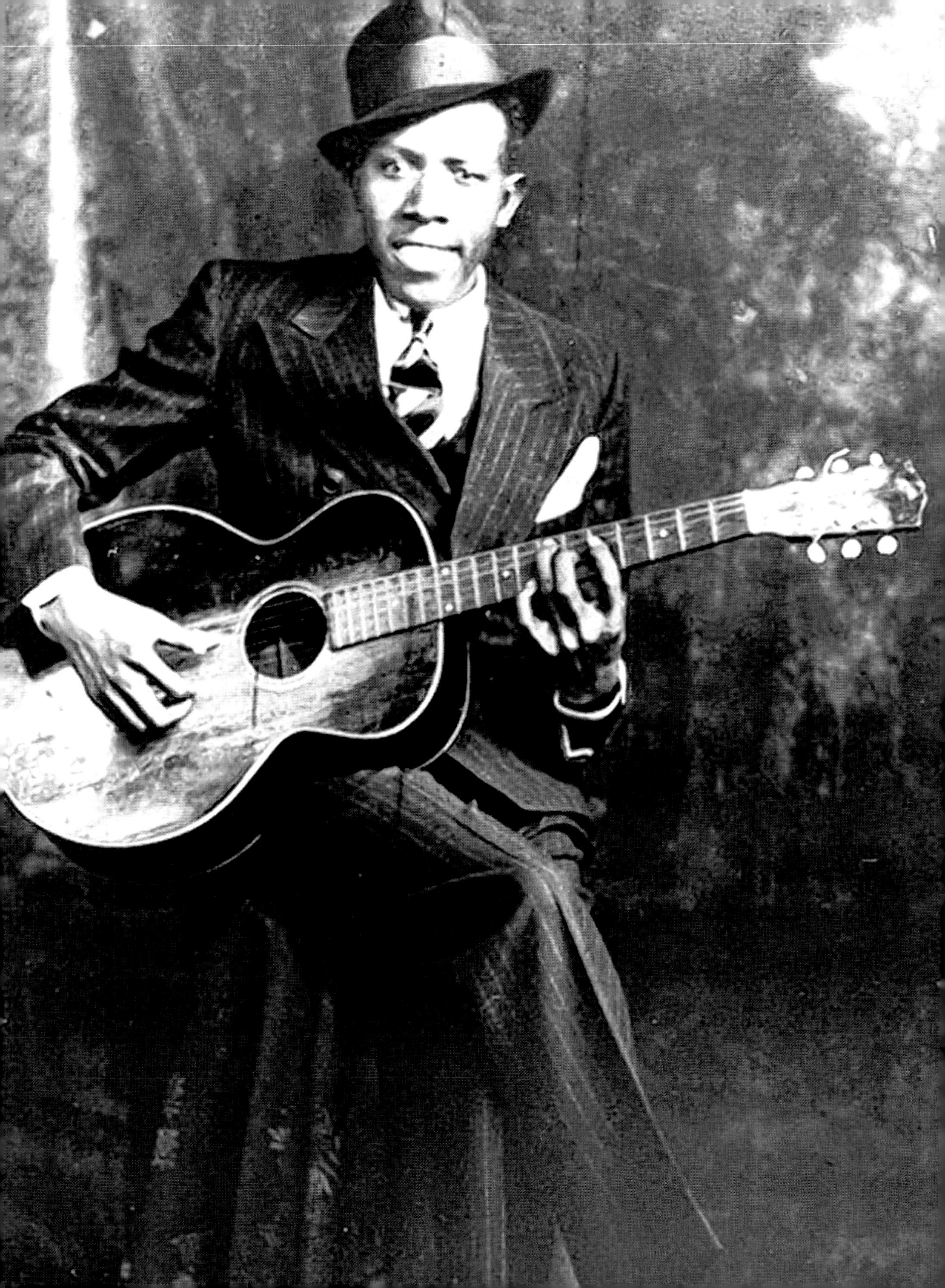

6

DEMONS IN POPULAR IMAGINATION

*"Me miserable! which way shall I fly
Infinite wrath, and infinite despair?
Which way I fly is Hell; myself am Hell;
And in the lowest deep a lower deep
Still threatening to devour me opens wide,
To which the Hell I suffer seems a Heav'n."*

JOHN MILTON, *PARADISE LOST*

DEMONS ARE NOT ONLY POPULAR subjects for ancient literature but also modern **folklore**. Folklore consists of many storytelling traditions shared within a community and spread through word of mouth. As rich as literature is as a source for stories about demons, folklore from cultures ranging from the United States to Japan offer an even deeper and more horrifying well of demon stories.

Robert Johnson: An All-American Faustus

An American folktale about demons surrounds the career and death of blues singer Robert Johnson. Johnson was born in 1911 and grew

Opposite: Blues singer Robert Johnson.

up on a plantation in the Mississippi Delta. From early on, Johnson seemed to have musical ambition, but he was a mediocre guitar player. One of Johnson's contemporaries, the musician Son House, said that audiences would often beg Johnson to quit playing his guitar during shows. Eventually, Johnson took their advice. For six months, he didn't play in Mississippi. At the end of that time, though, he returned to the stage, seeming to have mastered his instrument.

Seeing Johnson's meteoric rise to fame, many people started to suspect something. People at that time speculated that the source of Johnson's talent was unnatural. Stories differ, but the most widely told version of the story says that Johnson summoned the Devil at either a crossroads or a graveyard, two places commonly thought to host demonic spirits. There, Johnson was thought to have traded his soul in exchange for success in music, just as Dr. Faustus sold his soul to Mephistopheles in exchange for dark powers.

There would seem to be evidence to support this theory besides Johnson's curiously quick mastery of the guitar. For one, Johnson was only twenty-seven when he died, and his cause of death remains uncertain to this day. For those who believe the legend, Johnson died when the Devil came to him to uphold Johnson's end of the bargain. Furthermore, some hypothesize that Johnson himself may have confirmed the legend in one of his songs. Johnson's "Cross Road Blues" is full of fear and foreboding in part, people argue, because Johnson knows that his time is nearly up before the Devil will come to take his soul.

Japanese Urban Legends

The desolate crossroads and forests of America are not the only places haunted by demons. Even the highly sophisticated cities in

Japan are home to some terrifying **urban legends** about demonic spirits. An oni story that caught Japan by storm originated in the late 1970s. As the story goes, a woman was mutilated by her husband, who cut her mouth open with scissors. When she died, she became Kuchisake-Onna—the slit-mouthed woman. According to the legend, she will approach children wearing a surgeon's mask, which is commonly worn in Japan and other parts of Asia to protect against airborne diseases, and ask if they think she is pretty. If the child says yes, she will remove the mask, revealing her face, and ask again. If the child says no, Kuchisake-Onna cuts them in half out of rage. If the child says yes, she cuts the child's mouth with scissors to match hers. The only way to survive an encounter with Kuchisake-Onna is to give a vague answer, such as saying she looks average, or to distract her with fruits and candies.

People so feared Kuchisake-Onna when the legend first started circulating that many schools instituted a policy where students could only come to and from the campus in groups, many times only with teacher escorts. Police also increased patrols around schools to protect children.

La Pisadeira

Brazil is home to a particularly frightening demon that terrorizes people at night. *La pisadeira*, as she is known, is said to have long, yellowed nails and red eyes that glow while she hunts along the rooftops at night. After she has chosen a victim, she silently sneaks into their bedroom while they're asleep and pins them down in bed. When the person wakes up and sees the demon, la pisadeira watches them struggle as she feeds off their fear.

Fascinatingly, similar accounts of being held down in one's sleep by a malevolent force are told by many people, not just in Brazil, suggesting that the problem may not be supernatural but medical. Scientists believe that "la pisadeira" is a hallucination brought on by a disorder called sleep paralysis. One of the cycles that the brain goes through during sleep is called the "rapid eye movement," or REM, cycle. This is when dreams occur, but in order to prevent the body from acting out the dreams as if they were real, the brain shuts off the body's muscles. As the person wakens, his or her brain slowly allows the muscles to function again. (Sleepwalking is thought to be equal but opposite to sleep paralysis, in which the brain never engages in this paralysis, causing people to get up and walk around.) For people who suffer from sleep paralysis, this transition does not occur the way it should. In this case, the person wakes up to find that they cannot move or even call out for help—trapped in their own body.

Although sleep paralysis has been the topic of a great amount of research by sleep pathologists, or people who study sleep, there is still the question of what causes people to feel as though they are being targeted by an evil force. In addition to feelings of being restrained, there have been accounts of people seeing shadowy figures moving around the room, hearing scratches and other sounds, and even hearing sinister voices whispering in their ear.

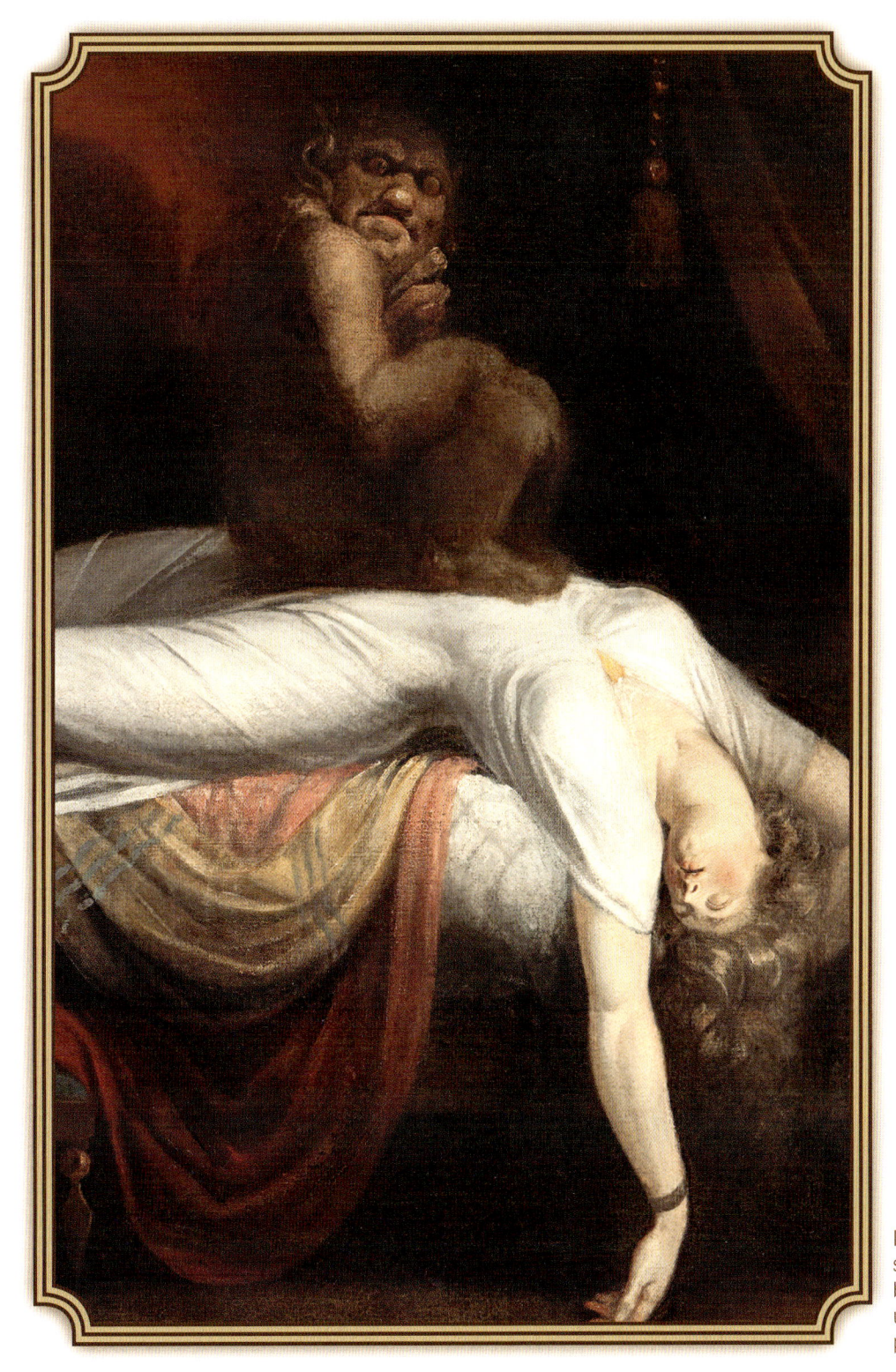

Demons are sometimes blamed for upsetting people's sleep.

The Pine Barrens of New Jersey.

The Jersey Devil

The Pine Barrens of New Jersey are a natural wonder. Although few people live in the heavily forested area encompassing seven counties in southern New Jersey, as the soil is too acidic to support conventional crops, it is home to many different species of plants and animals. This diversity of life is just one of the reasons Congress chose the Pine Barrens as the United States' first National Reserve. However, there may be another creature lurking among the pines: the Jersey Devil.

The Jersey Devil (or, as it is known to locals, the Leeds Devil) is a creature whose legend dates back to the colonial era. In the early 1700s, a woman named Leeds was the mother to twelve children. As the story goes, she became pregnant with a thirteenth. Mrs. Leeds was exasperated by her repeated pregnancies, and when she went into labor on a stormy night, she screamed, "May this one be the Devil!" One version of the story holds that Leeds was a witch and the father of the baby was the Devil himself. Another says that Leeds had upset a gypsy, who cursed the baby. In any event, the child was born normally, but started to change form shortly after. Its skin turned to scales, its feet to talons. Bats' wings sprouted from its back, a forked tail sprang from its bottom, and its face turned into that of a horse. It crashed around the room, killing the midwife helping Leeds with the birth, before flying up the chimney.

The Jersey Devil is said to haunt southern New Jersey to this day. Sightings have been recorded as recently as October 2015, when a resident of Little Egg Harbor Township captured a photo of a furry, horned creature resembling a goat flying through the air. The Devil has been a source of pride for New Jerseyans and lends its name to the state's NHL team, the New Jersey Devils.

WILLIAM PETER BLATTY'S
THE EXORCIST
DIRECTED BY WILLIAM FRIEDKIN

ELLEN BURSTYN   MAX VON SYDOW   LEE J. COBB   KITTY WINN   JACK MacGOWRAN   JASON MILLER AS FATHER KARRAS   LINDA BLAIR AS REGAN
PRODUCED BY WILLIAM PETER BLATTY   EXECUTIVE PRODUCER NOEL MARSHALL   SCREENPLAY BY WILLIAM PETER BLATTY   BASED ON HIS NOVEL

R RESTRICTED
UNDER 17 REQUIRES ACCOMPANYING PARENT OR ADULT GUARDIAN

www.theexorcist.net   New Digitally Restored Sound

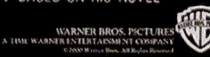

WARNER BROS. PICTURES
A TIME WARNER ENTERTAINMENT COMPANY

7

DEMONS IN THE MODERN WORLD

"The Devil is precise; the marks of his presence are definite as stone."

ARTHUR MILLER, *THE CRUCIBLE*

DEMONS CONTINUE TO HAVE RELEVANCE today. In the developed parts of the world, including the United States, Canada, and Europe, the popular opinion of demons is complicated. For many skeptics, demons are fictional monsters best left to the imagination of horror movie directors. For others, demons continue to pose a real spiritual threat.

Pop Culture Demons

Movies about demons and the Devil are extremely popular. Movies such as *The Exorcist* (directed by William Friedkin, 1973), *The Omen* (directed by Richard Donner, 1976), and *Rosemary's Baby* (directed by Roman Polanski, 1968), all of which are based on

Opposite: The movie poster for *The Exorcist.*

demon possession and the **occult**, are frequently chosen for lists of the scariest movies of all time. The Exorcist has a particularly frightening reputation, as both fans and movie critics frequently name it as the scariest movie of all time.

Demons also make an appearance on television in shows like *Supernatural*. First aired in 2005, *Supernatural* tells the story of Sam (played by Jared Padalecki) and Dean (played by Jensen Ackles) Winchester, two human brothers who hunt paranormal entities and occult forces. In addition to battling creatures such as ghosts, vampires, and ancient gods, Sam and Dean must explore the disappearance of their father and the mysterious death of their mother at the hands of demons. Along the way, Sam and Dean become the focus of a war between angels and demons.

The Constant Threat of Evil

Although the Catholic Church has developed what may be the most organized approach to expelling demon possession over its centuries of existence, for the last few decades it has in large part been moving away from recognizing the importance of the ritual. This is in part because many Catholics believe that the Devil is not a real concern in daily life. For many Catholics, exorcism is considered to be an outdated ritual that has little relevance today. While the Devil and his army of demons had been considered very real threats in the Middle Ages, many Catholic priests, especially in the United States and Europe, have been preaching that demons are a more figurative threat. Very recently, however, Pope Francis, the religion's newest head who was named in 2013, seems to be reviving belief in actual evil spirits and the importance in the ancient rite.

To Pope Francis, the head of the Roman Catholic Church, demons are a very real threat even in the modern world.

Pope Francis was originally a member of the Jesuits. In addition to being the order of priests who performed the exorcism of Roland Doe in the 1940s, the Jesuits were founded on the motivation to help ease the actual struggle of people in the real world. To Jesuits, it is not enough to simply offer spiritual consolation or comfort; Jesuit priests are also called to try to ease people's physical suffering. Given this, it is no wonder that Pope Francis is trying to revive concern over the real threat posed by demons. During a Mass in the Vatican, Pope Francis told those assembled to "look out, because the Devil is present." Pope Francis sees exorcism as another tool in the Catholic Church's arsenal to provide relief to those who are suffering.

According to the *Washington Post,* requests for exorcisms are on the rise, especially in countries where the predominant religion is Catholicism. Cardinals in Milan and Turin, Italy, and Madrid, Spain, are looking to expand its ranks of qualified exorcists. This is especially surprising because the number of people who identify as Catholic has been declining in recent years.

Occult Religions

One reason the Catholic Church is looking to increase the number of exorcists is because of a perceived rise in the number of mystical cults and their believers. Many of these cults are based on medieval notions of sorcery and witchcraft as well as even more ancient pagan beliefs and rituals. An example of these occult religions is Wicca, which is the largest neopagan (or "new pagan") spirituality.

Compared to Christianity and other popular religions, Wicca is highly individualistic and lacks many of the features of an organized religion. In fact, Wiccans (those who practice Wicca) say that it isn't a religion at all but rather a spirituality. Because Wiccans are free to explore their beliefs as they choose, there is a great variety in the ways Wiccans practice this spirituality. Nevertheless, Wicca does have some general teachings that are shared by its practitioners, including a respect for nature and a belief in the power of magic rituals.

Wiccans are often confused with Satanists, who practice another occult religion that worships Satan and other dark spirits. Both Wiccans and Satanists use symbols commonly associated with the Devil, including five-sided stars called pentagrams and images of a horned deity that resembles popular representations of Satan.

Occult religions such as Wicca often use mystical symbols such as the pentagram, which many consider to be strange or demonic.

However, unlike Satanists, who celebrate Lucifer challenging the control God had over him, Wicca holds that Lucifer is just one of a number of fabrications made by organized religions to prevent people from expressing their spirituality.

Regardless of these distinctions, many people fear Wiccans, Satanists, and other pagan religions because of their use of occult symbols and rituals that have been associated with dark, evil forces throughout history. While people fear these symbols, people like

Wiccans find peace and power in them. Just as new religions have often replaced older ones and made their demons out to that religion's gods, Wiccans and others like them are attempting to reclaim those ancient gods and powers.

Demons of Rock

Many modern rock musicians often make explicit connections with demons and the Devil. Many songs make mention of the occult, including some of the most popular songs of all time, including Iron Maiden's "The Number of the Beast," Van Halen's "Runnin' with the Devil," and the Rolling Stones' "Sympathy for the Devil," to name a few. Other bands, especially heavy metal bands, choose occult imagery and references for everything from their merchandise to their group's name. Seas of crowds flashing "devil horns," formed by extending the index and pinky fingers, are a common sight at many rock concerts.

When rock first came onto the scene in the 1950s, many conservatives in American culture were shocked by the aggressive beats and suggestive themes of the music, as well as the gyrating dance moves of rock stars, such as Elvis Presley. This led many people to argue that rock music was literally Satan's music. Many fundamentalist Christians have argued that rock music contains subliminal messages that influence listeners toward everything from drug use to Devil worship. Many pastors came forward with evidence claiming that certain songs played backwards included Satanic chants. However, many audiologists (people who study how people hear) have shown these to be cases of audio pareidolia, where a person's brain mistakenly registers words in strings of sounds.

Today, fans sometimes use symbols such as devil horns to show they like a certain band.

The reason musicians use the occult are numerous. In many instances, such as "Sympathy for the Devil," the Devil is used as a lens to consider what about human nature led to some of the darkest moments in history, such as the crucifixion of Jesus, the Nazi blitzkrieg, and the assassination of John F. Kennedy. In other cases, occult symbolism is used as a sort of signifier of rebellion, a common theme in rock music.

The Nature of Evil

With the great variety of cultures and beliefs in the world today, there is a fresh debate about the nature of true evil. What one group finds frightening, another might find comforting. Fear is a personal experience that cannot be fully shared or even understood by another. It is here in our sense of isolation that demons have and will continue to lurk: in the wilderness of the forest, in the loneliness of the desert, in the haunting echoes of an abandoned place, and in the dark parts of the world and of our minds that we dare not venture into.

Glossary

damnation The soul's condemnation to reside in eternal punishment.

demon An evil spirit.

demonology The study of demons.

Devil The primary evil spirit in Judeo-Christian mythology; also called Satan or Lucifer.

djinn A type of spirit in Arabian and Islamic mythology that is able to appear to humans, grant wishes, and possess human bodies; also called a *jinn* or genie.

exorcism The act of expelling an evil spirit, especially from a person.

folklore The traditional beliefs of a community spread through word of mouth.

Hell The place in many religious and mythological traditions where evil souls are punished for eternity.

Jesuit A member of a religious order within the Roman Catholic Church.

malevolent Evil.

necromancy Evil or "black" magic, in which a person summons someone from the dead.

occult Supernatural or magical beliefs and practices.

oni Japanese demons. Oni have roots in Chinese and Buddhist myths and are often illustrated as huge creatures with red skin and horns.

pitchfork A farming tool with approximately three sharp metal prongs at the end of a long handle used for lifting hay.

possess (demonic) The state where a demon or other spirit takes complete control over a person's body.

rakshasa A demon in the Hindu religion, said to be a cannibalistic spirit that hunts humans at night.

schizophrenia A mental disorder characterized by severe delusions as a result of a person's mental disintegration.

succubus A malevolent female spirit that preys on sleeping men.

Tanakh The fundamental text of the Jewish religion.

urban legend A story about an unusual event or occurrence whose origin is unknown; usually passed through word of mouth.

witchcraft The practice of magic, especially evil or black magic, through spells and the invitation of demonic spirits.

To Learn More About Demons

Books

Clarke, Roger. *Ghosts: A Natural History: 500 Years of Searching for Proof.* New York: St. Martin's Press, 2012.

Guiley, Rosemary Ellen. *The Encyclopedia of Demons and Demonology.* New York: Checkmark Books, 2009.

Marlowe, Christopher. *Dr. Faustus.* New York: Dover Thrift Editions, 1994.

Website

DeliriumsRealm
www.deliriumsrealm.com
DeliriumsRealm features articles on a variety of topics associated with demons and demonology.

Television Show

Supernatural
Created by Eric Kripke, this TV series follows brothers Sam and Dean Winchester as they hunt paranormal creatures from a variety of cultures, including demons. Make sure to get your parents' permission before tuning in, however, as the show is rated TV-14 for language, suggestive themes, and some frightening scenes.

Bibliography

Aquinas, St. Thomas. "Question 97: The Punishment of the Damned." *Summa Theologica*. New Advent.org. Accessed November 22, 2015. http://www.newadvent.org/summa/5097.htm.

Clarke, Roger. *Ghosts: A Natural History: 500 Years of Searching for Proof*. New York: St. Martin's Press, 2012.

DeliriumsRealm. Accessed November 22, 2015. http://www.deliriumsrealm.com.

DeRosa, Victoria. "10 Horrifying Demons and Spirits from Japanese Folklore." Mental Floss.com. Accessed November 22, 2015. http://mentalfloss.com/article/59737/10-horrifying-demons-and-spirits-japanese-folklore.

Guiley, Rosemary Ellen. *The Encyclopedia of Demons and Demonology*. New York: Checkmark Books, 2009.

"Jewish Concepts: Demons and Demonology." Jewish Virtual Library. Accessed November 22, 2015. http://www.jewishvirtuallibrary.org/jsource/Judaism/demons.html.

"Lost Tapes Wendigo." Animal Planet.com. Accessed November 22, 2015. http://www.animalplanet.com/tv-shows/lost-tapes/creatures/wendigo.

Marlowe, Christopher. *Doctor Faustus*. Edited by David Wootton. Indianapolis: Hackett Classics, 2005.

Rose, Joel. "Robert Johnson At 100, Still Dispelling Myths." NPR.org. Accessed November 22, 2015. http://www.npr.org/2011/05/07/136063911/robert-johnson-at-100-still-dispelling-myths.

Ruset, Ben. "The Legend of the Jersey Devil. NJ Pine Barrens.com. Accessed November 22, 2015. http://www.njpinebarrens.com/the-legend-of-the-jersey-devil.

Tomlinson, Simon. "The Devil in Roland Doe: How the 1973 horror film The Exorcist was based on a real-life possession in Missouri." *Daily Mail*. Accessed November 22, 2015. http://www.dailymail.co.uk/news/article-2449423/Devil-Roland-Doe-The-Exorcist-based-real-life-Missouri-possession.html.

Index

Page numbers in **boldface** are illustrations. Entries in **boldface** are glossary terms.

Aladdin, 16–17
angels, 10–11, 15, 33–34, **36**, 54
    Lucifer, 10–11, 32, 57

Bible, 12, 17, 25
Buddhism, 19

Christianity, **8**, 10, 12–13, 15, 17–19, 23, 35, 56, 58

damnation, 34
demonology, 10, 17
Devil, 11, 13, **13**, 15, 23–25, 33–35, 38, 42, 46, 53–56, 58–59
djinn, 16, **16**
dybbuk, 18

exorcism, **26**, 39–42, 54–56

Faustian bargain, 34
folklore, 45

genie, 16–18, 25
gods, 10, 13, 19, 54, 58
golem, 18

Hell, **8**, 11–13, **12**, 24, 26, 33
Hinduism, 18–19

Islam, 15–16, 18

Jersey Devil, 51
Jesuit, 42, 55
Johnson, Robert, **44**, 45–46
Judaism, 15, 17, 21, 35

malevolent, 10, 19, 48

necromancy, 32

occult, 54, 56–59
oni, 20, **20**, 47
Ouija board, 41–43

pitchfork, 13, **13**
possess, 18, 25–29, 39–41, 54

rakshasa, 19, **19**
Roman Catholic, 10–11, 37–38

Satan, 11, 13, 35, 56, 58
schizophrenia, 27
succubus, 21
supernatural, 9–10, 48

Tanakh, 17, 21

urban legend, 46–47

wendigo, 28–29
Wiccan, 56–58
witchcraft, 17, 35, 56

About the Author

Andrew Coddington earned a degree in creative writing from Canisius College. He formerly worked in publishing as an editor. He has written several books, including *Ghosts* and *Aliens* in the Creatures of Fantasy series. Andrew lives in Lancaster, New York, behind a forest that he hopes isn't haunted.